The 25 Rules t

MW01052190

1 Sentences 3
A sentence is a whole thought.

2 Sentences 7
A sentence begins with a capital letter.

3 Telling Sentences 11
A sentence that tells something needs
a period at the end.

4 Asking Sentences 15
A sentence that asks something needs
a question mark at the end.

5 Pronoun *I* 19
The word *I* is always capitalized.

6 Proper Nouns (People and Pets) 23
The names of people and pets begin with
capital letters.

7 Proper Nouns (Places) 27
The names of specific places begin with
capital letters.

8 Proper Nouns (Days of the Week) 31
The names of the days of the week begin
with capital letters.

9 Proper Nouns (Months) 35
The names of the months begin with
capital letters.

10 Proper Nouns (Holidays) 39
The names of holidays begin with capital letters.

11 Nouns 43
Some words name things.

12 Verbs 47
Some words tell what is happening or what
already happened.

13 Pronouns 51
Some words take the place of names.
These words are called pronouns.

14 Contractions 55
A contraction is a short way to write two words.

15 Contractions 59
A contraction uses an apostrophe.

16 Compound Words 63
Two words can sometimes be put together
to make a new word. These words are called
compound words.

17 Using *I* & *Me* 67
Use *I* when you are the person doing something.
Use *me* when something happens to you.

18 Using *We* & *Us* 71
Use *we* when you and other people do
something. Use *us* when something
happens to you and other people.

19 Using *They* & *Them* 75
Use *they* when several people do something.
Use *them* when something happens to
several people.

20 Plural Nouns (Add *s*) 79
Add *s* to most nouns to name more than one.

21 Plural Nouns (Add *es*) 83
Add *es* to some nouns to show more than one.

22 Using *Is* & *Are* 87
Use *is* with one and *are* with more than one.

23 Possessives 91
When something belongs to one person,
add *'s* to the name of the person.

24 Past Tense 95
Some words add *ed* to tell that something
has already happened.

25 Irregular Verbs 99
Some special words show that something
has already happened.

About the Book

Grammar & Punctuation includes:

25 Rule Charts
Use the charts to introduce the rules. Choose the rules and the order of use that is appropriate to your students' needs.

Student Practice Pages
Each rule is supported by 3 scaffolded, reproducible practice pages. Use the level that is appropriate for your students. The pages may be used with the whole class or as independent practice. They are also useful as homework review.

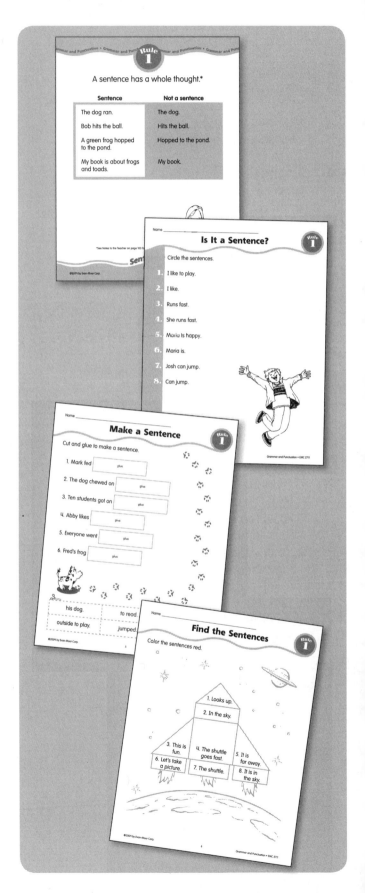

A sentence is a whole thought.*

Sentence	Not a sentence
The dog ran.	The dog
Bob hits the ball.	Hits the ball.
A green frog hopped to the pond.	Hopped to the pond.
My book is about frogs and toads.	My book.

*See Notes to the Teacher on page 103 for additional information.

Sentences

Is It a Sentence?

Circle the sentences.

1. I like to play.

2. I like.

3. Runs fast.

4. She runs fast.

5. Maria is happy.

6. Maria is.

7. Josh can jump.

8. Can jump.

Make a Sentence

Cut and glue to make a sentence.

1. Mark fed

   glue

2. The dog chewed on

   glue

3. Ten students got on

   glue

4. Abby likes

   glue

5. Everyone went

   glue

6. Fred's frog

   glue

his dog.	to read.	the bus.
outside to play.	jumped.	a bone.

Find the Sentences

Color the sentences red.

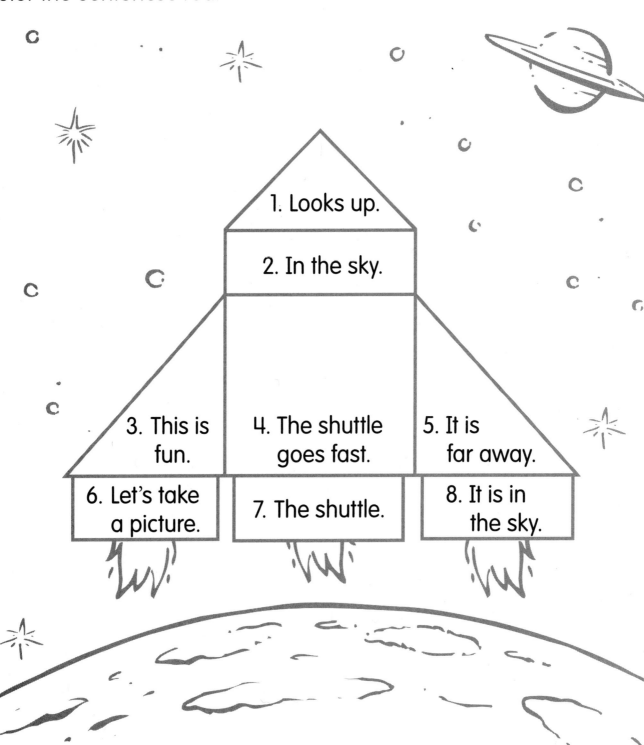

1. Looks up.

2. In the sky.

3. This is fun.

4. The shuttle goes fast.

5. It is far away.

6. Let's take a picture.

7. The shuttle.

8. It is in the sky.

A sentence begins with a capital letter.

The box is red.

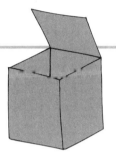

Jan has a pet cat.

This flower is pretty.

Sentences

A Good Beginning

Circle the sentences that begin with a capital letter.
Fix the sentences that do **not** begin with a capital letter.

1. Mike fed the animals.

2. the cow is in the field.

3. ana likes horses.

4. The pigs are eating.

5. Chickens are running.

6. my cat is sleeping.

7. The dog is chasing a butterfly.

8. We named the goat Whiskers.

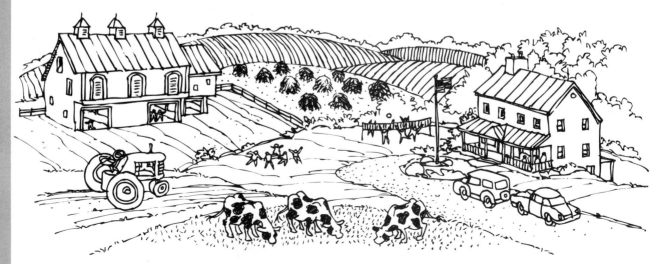

Capital Letters

Fix the words that need capital letters.

1. her rabbit is brown.

2. My rabbit has a white tail.

3. the rabbits are hopping.

4. Let's play with the rabbits.

5. look at his long ears.

6. he has a cute nose.

7. Sue feeds her rabbit.

8. we named the rabbit Fluffy.

Yes or No?

Does the sentence begin with a capital letter?

1. Let's make some cookies.   **yes**   **no**

2. we will need a bowl and a spoon.   **yes**   **no**

3. Measure one cup of sugar.   **yes**   **no**

4. Add an egg.   **yes**   **no**

5. mix it up.   **yes**   **no**

6. turn on the oven.   **yes**   **no**

7. Cut out cookie shapes.   **yes**   **no**

8. put them in the oven.   **yes**   **no**

A sentence that tells something needs a period (.) at the end.

See the fat cat.

The bell rang.

Six children
sang a song.

Telling Sentences

End with a Period

Find each sentence. Put a period at the end. Color the bone.

1. I have four legs

2. Run and play

3. My tail wags when I am happy

4. A ball for me

5. Sometimes, Spot

6. My name is Spot

Mixed-Up Sentences

Unscramble the words. End each sentence with a period.

1. soccer plays Eric

_____

2. to the zoo went I

_____

3. Sam sunflowers planted

_____

4. jump can rope They

_____

Name _____

Add the Ending

Fill in the blanks. End each sentence with a period.

school Sara ball sky bike bone flower wheels

1. He walked to _____

2. My dog eats a _____

3. They like to play _____

4. My friend's name is _____

5. She can ride a _____

6. The clouds are in the _____

7. My bike has two _____

8. Look at that pretty _____

Rule 4

A sentence that asks something needs a question mark (?) at the end.

Do you want a cookie?

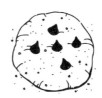

Will you play with me?

Why are you crying?

Asking Sentences

Is It a Question?

End each asking sentence with a question mark.
End each telling sentence with a period.

1. How many students are here today

2. There are 25 students here today

3. The rug is dirty

4. What happened to the rug

5. Did you make that model car

6. What color will you paint your car

7. Do we have any milk

8. I put milk on my cereal

Asking or Telling?

Rule
4

Cut and group.

Asking Sentences	**Telling Sentences**

glue	glue
glue	glue
glue	glue

Do you have a pet mouse?	I have a pet mouse.	We can play a game.
Would you like to play?	Is your name Mike?	Your name is Mike.

Asking Sentences

Add question marks at the end of sentences that ask
something. Answer the questions with a telling sentence.
Be sure to use a period after your answer.

1. How many sisters do you have ?

_____

2. Your home has two floors

_____

3. Do you have any pets

_____

4. What is your favorite fruit

_____

The word **I** is always capitalized.

I like to eat.

Ann and **I** went to the park.

When **I** was born, **I** had blue eyes.

Pronoun I

The I Search

Circle the sentences that have a capital **I**. Fix the sentences that do **not** have a capital **I**.

1. Joel and I are friends.

2. i can ride a horse.

3. I can draw a picture.

4. That is the game i like to play.

5. i like that monkey.

6. I will eat an apple.

7. Maria and I like that kitten.

8. i like the circus.

I Did It

Write a capital **I** in the blanks.

1. _____ went to the store.

2. Where did _____ put that toy?

3. _____ ate lunch with a friend.

4. _____ read ten pages in that book.

5. This is where _____ spilled the drink.

6. _____ named the fish Fred.

7. _____ bought a computer game.

8. _____ can draw a horse.

Name _____

What I Like

Color the picture next to each sentence that has a capital **I**.

1. I like to play ball.

2. Sue and i like to read.

3. I have a pet bird.

4. May I have a cookie?

5. I can swim.

6. Am i pretty?

     Grammar and Punctuation • EMC 2711

The names of people and pets begin with capital letters.

Marcus	**A**my	**S**amuel
Mr. **M**iller	**M**s. **H**ill	**D**r. **R**ose
Sparky	**F**luff	**S**nowball

Proper Nouns

Name Tags

The names of people begin with capital letters.
Fix the name tags.

Melissa

terry

oscar

Ruth

Ali

Yoshi

carl

Felipe

The Name Game

Write a name for each person. Begin each name with a capital letter.

1. a girl _____

2. a boy _____

3. a pet _____

4. a teacher _____

5. a friend _____

6. a neighbor _____

7. a person on television _____

8. a person in a book _____

Name That Person

Fill in the blanks with names. Begin each name with a capital letter.

1. _____ and _____ are my friends.

2. _____ is a fast runner.

3. I like to sit with _____.

4. _____ is tall.

5. _____ is wearing a blue shirt.

6. _____ has a pet named _____.

7. _____ and _____ like to read.

8. _____ is wearing running shoes.

Rule 7

The names of specific places begin with capital letters.

state	**N**ew **Y**ork
street	**E**lm **S**treet
city	**D**allas
country	**U**nited **S**tates of **A**merica
park	**Y**ellowstone **N**ational **P**ark
school	**B**ayview **E**lementary

Proper Nouns

Circle the Names

Circle the words that are names of specific places.

1. park   Central Park

2. Utah   state

3. Miami   city

4. The Great Mall   mall

5. street   Main Street

6. zoo   Los Angeles Zoo

7. Disneyland   amusement park

8. river   Amazon River

Name the Places

Answer the questions.

1. What is the name of your school?

_____

2. What is the name of the state you live in?

_____

3. What city or town do you live in?

_____

4. What is the name of the street you live on?

_____

Name _____

Special Places

Rule
7

Color the words that are the names of specific places.

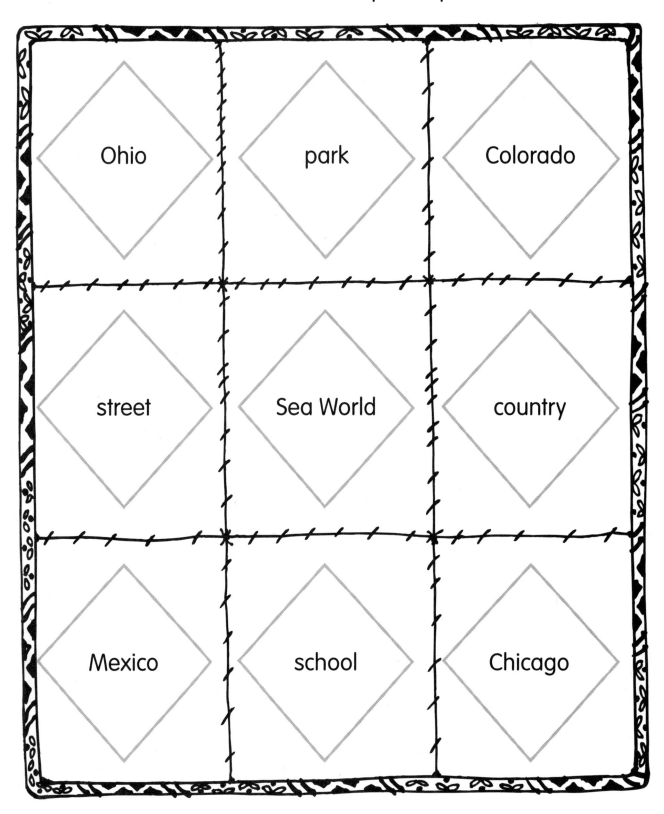

Ohio   park   Colorado

street   Sea World   country

Mexico   school   Chicago

The names of the days of the week begin with capital letters.

Sunday

Monday

Tuesday

Wednesday

Thursday

Friday

Saturday

Proper Nouns

Name _____

Seven Days a Week

Circle the days of the week.
Fix the days of the week that do **not** begin with a capital letter.

1. sunday is the first day of the week.

2. Monday we go to school.

3. I will play in the park on thursday.

4. I watch television on Tuesday.

5. I have a soccer game on Saturday.

6. My friend can play on wednesday.

7. My birthday is on Friday.

8. I will return this book on monday.

November

Sunday	Monday	Tuesday	Wednesday	Thursday	Friday	Saturday
1	2	3	4	5	6	7
8	9	10	11	12	13	14
15	16	17	18	19	20	21
22	23	24	25	26	27	28
29	30					

The Order of the Days

Write the days of the week in the correct order.

1. _____Sunday_____

2. _____

3. _____

4. _____

5. _____

6. _____

7. _____

Name _____

What Day Is It?

Write a day of the week in each blank.

1. _____ starts with the letter **W**.

2. School is closed on _____ and

_____.

3. The day after Thursday is _____.

4. _____ is the day before Tuesday.

5. _____ and _____ start

with the letter **T**.

Rule 9

The names of the months begin with capital letters.

January	**J**uly
February	**A**ugust
March	**S**eptember
April	**O**ctober
May	**N**ovember
June	**D**ecember

Proper Nouns

Name _____

Months of the Year

Circle the months of the year. Fix the months that do **not** begin with a capital letter.

1. A flower bloomed in (M)may.

2. We will go on a trip in July.

3. I will visit my grandmother in april.

4. My favorite month is december.

5. The month of march has 31 days.

6. The first month of the year is January.

7. My school started in august.

8. My school will end in June.

Months in Order

Write the months in order.

1. _____, February, _____

2. April, _____, June

3. _____, _____, September

4. October, _____, December

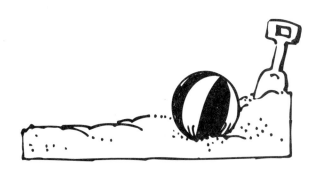

37

Month Facts

Rule 9

Write the name of a month in each blank.

1. My birthday is in the month of _____.

2. Mother's Day is in the month of _____.

3. Father's Day is in the month of _____.

4. The first month of the year is _____.

5. _____ is the last month of the year.

6. My favorite month is _____.

7. _____ is a month in the summer.

8. Thanksgiving is in the month of _____.

Rule 10

The names of holidays begin with capital letters.

Thanksgiving

Independence **D**ay

Presidents' **D**ay

St. **P**atrick's **D**ay

Chinese **N**ew **Y**ear

Proper Nouns

Name _____

Holidays

Circle the holidays. Draw a line under each capital letter.

1. We watch football games on New Year's Day.

2. Flag Day is in June.

3. I went to a party on Valentine's Day.

4. On Groundhog Day, the sun was shining.

5. Our town has a parade on Memorial Day.

6. My class put on a play for Martin Luther King, Jr. Day.

7. On the Fourth of July, we had a picnic.

8. School starts after Labor Day.

Holiday Letters

Fill in the missing capital letters.

1. ___olumbus ___ay

2. ___wanzaa

3. ___eterans ___ay

4. ___other's ___ay

5. ___arth ___ay

6. ___ather's ___ay

7. ___alloween

8. ___rbor ___ay

Columbus Day	Kwanzaa	Veterans Day
Mother's Day	Earth Day	Father's Day
Halloween	Arbor Day	

Name _____

Favorite Holidays

Write the name of the holiday that goes with each picture.

Thanksgiving	Halloween	Fourth of July
St. Patrick's Day	Easter	Valentine's Day

1.  _____

2.  _____

3. _____

4.  _____

5. _____

6.  _____

　　　42　　　Grammar and Punctuation • EMC 2711

Some words name things.

The **turtle** is in its **shell**.

A **hen** laid an **egg**.

The **sun** is hot.
The **moon** is not hot.

Nouns

Noun Search

Color each balloon that names something.

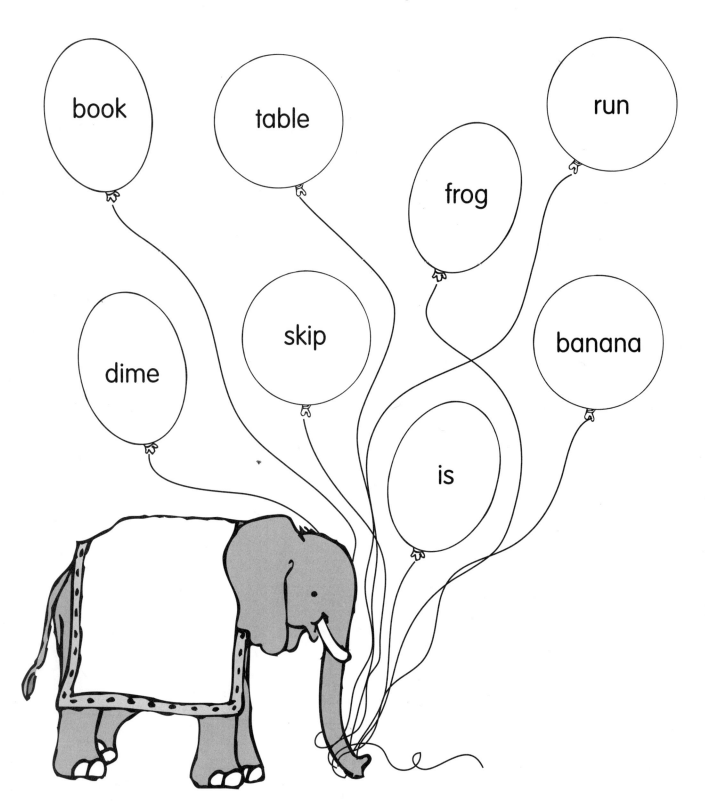

book

table

run

frog

skip

banana

dime

is

Find the Nouns

Circle the words that name something.

1. That is my pig.

2. Here is some ice cream.

3. Put the paper on the desk.

4. This is my pencil.

5. There is an apple in the bag.

6. The candy tasted good.

7. Put the flowers on the table.

8. These shoes are white.

Write the Nouns

Write words that name something.

1. Put the _____ in the yard.

2. What color is your _____?

3. I found a _____ on the sidewalk.

4. I like to play _____.

5. I like to eat _____.

6. There is a _____ in the box.

7. That _____ is pretty.

8. My favorite subject in school is _____.

Rule 12

Some words tell what is happening or what already happened.

What is happening:

Dan **rides** his bike to school.

I **write** with a pencil.

What already happened:

The dog **jumped** on the chair.

The baby **slept**.

Verbs

The Verb Hunt

Color the words that tell what is happening or what already happened.

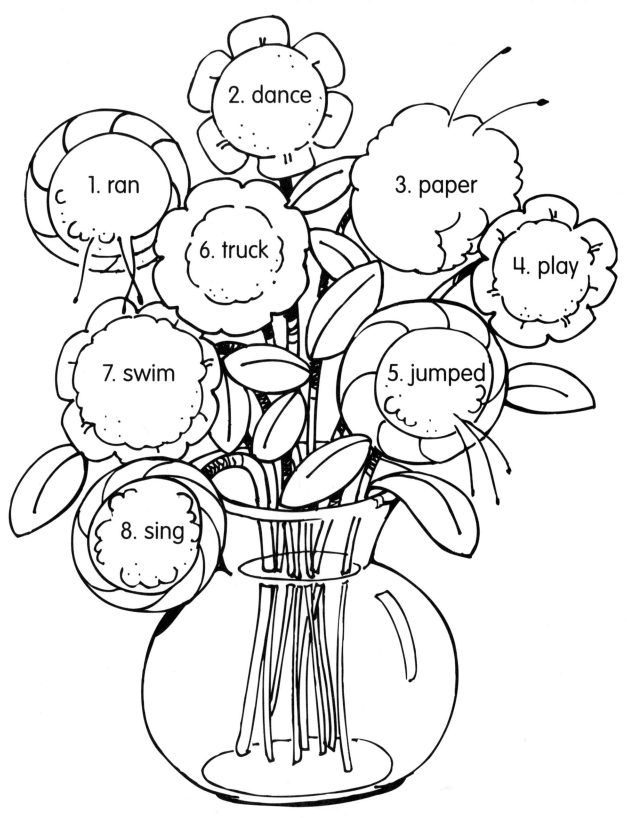

Find the Verbs

Circle the words that tell what is happening or what already happened.

1. He walks to school.

2. Lisa ran up the hill.

3. Ben planted carrots.

4. The dog chased the cat.

5. She sang a song.

6. The bird sits in the nest.

7. He tells his teacher a story.

8. The baby sleeps in a crib.

la la la la la laaaa!

Pick a Verb

Fill in the blanks.

barked   drank   swim   ran   rode   hopped   sat   read

1. The dog _____.

2. The fish like to _____.

3. The mouse _____ around.

4. The students _____ in chairs.

5. I _____ a glass of water.

6. He _____ his bike.

7. She likes to _____ books.

8. The bunny _____ on the grass.

Rule 13

Some words take the place of names. These words are called pronouns.

Ben goes to school.

He is in first grade.

Ann has a kitten.

She takes care of **it**.

Shannon and I are good friends.

We play games together.

Marcia and Carlos are dancers.

They take lessons on Saturday.

Pronouns

Name _____

Write the Pronouns

Rule
13

Write pronouns in the blanks for the underlined words.

them	We	it	He	She	They

1. <u>Cory</u> can run fast.

_____ can run fast.

2. <u>Jill and Meg</u> went for a walk.

_____ went for a walk.

3. <u>Ann</u> has a <u>bike</u>.

_____ rides _____ to school.

4. <u>Leo and I</u> baked some <u>cookies</u>.

_____ will eat some of _____.

Which Pronoun?

Fill in the blanks.

| I | He | She | We | They |

1. _____ am going to the store.

2. _____ was the first girl to finish the race.

3. _____ were happy to finish the race.

4. _____ is taking a nap.

5. _____ are playing tag.

6. _____ am going camping.

7. _____ is going to the library.

8. _____ was the first boy in line.

I am a bear.

Use a Pronoun

Rewrite the sentences using pronouns for the underlined words.

We	He	They	She

1. <u>Kay</u> ate some cake.

_____

2. <u>Jim and Hugo</u> went to the lake.

_____

3. <u>Bob</u> has a red boat.

_____

4. <u>Alice and I</u> like to run.

_____

Rule 14

A contraction is a short way to write two words.

can not	**can't**
is not	**isn't**
I have	**I've**
I am	**I'm**
it is	**it's**
that is	**that's**
we are	**we're**
she is	**she's**
they will	**they'll**
they are	**they're**

Contractions

Make a Match

Match each contraction with the two words that were used
to make it.

don't	can not
can't	let us
I'll	do not
wasn't	did not
it's	are not
didn't	I will
let's	was not
aren't	there is
there's	it is

The Missing Letters

Write the contraction.

1. she is = ___ ___ ___ ' ___

2. that is = ___ ___ ___ ___ ' ___

3. have not = ___ ___ ___ ___ ___ ' ___

4. we will = ___ ___ ' ___ ___

5. you will = ___ ___ ___ ' ___ ___

6. is not = ___ ___ ___ ' ___

7. I have = ___ ' ___ ___

8. they are = ___ ___ ___ ___ ' ___ ___

What Two Words?

Write the words for each contraction.

1. didn't _____ and _____

2. don't _____ and _____

3. it's _____ and _____

4. I'll _____ and _____

5. couldn't _____ and _____

6. can't _____ and _____

7. he's _____ and _____

8. I'm _____ and _____

Rule 15

A contraction uses an apostrophe (').

don't	it's
I'll	let's
couldn't	he's
she'll	that's

Contractions

Name _____

The Missing Apostrophe

Fill in the missing apostrophe.

1. c a n t

2. i t s

3. h a v e n t

4. I l l

5. I v e

6. h e s

7. d i d n t

8. t h a t s

Make Contractions

Write the contraction.

1. where is _____

2. what is _____

3. you have _____

4. we are _____

5. I would _____

6. you are _____

7. is not _____

8. I am _____

Contractions in Sentences

Rewrite the sentences using contractions for the underlined words.

1. <u>She is</u> flying a kite.

_____

2. <u>What is</u> your name?

_____

3. <u>They are</u> having fun.

_____

4. Please <u>do not</u> run in the house.

_____

5. He <u>does not</u> ride the bus.

_____

Rule 16

Two words can sometimes be put together to make a new word. These words are called compound words.

pan + cake = **pancake**

butter + fly = **butterfly**

base + ball = **baseball**

cow + boy = **cowboy**

Compound Words

Put It Together

Write each compound word.

1. foot + ball = _____

2. skate + board = _____

3. birth + day = _____

4. air + plane = _____

5. flash + light = _____

6. some + thing = _____

7. every + one = _____

8. dog + house = _____

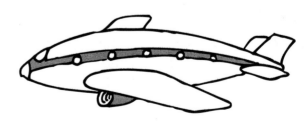

Make a Match

Match the words to make compound words.

sun	fish
gold	father
pop	flower
grand	corn
sea	road
any	shell
rail	one

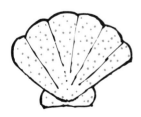

Make a Word

Cut and glue to make compound words.

after [glue]	side [glue]
base [glue]	over [glue]
rain [glue]	every [glue]

✂ -

noon	walk	ball
bow	night	thing

Use **I** when you are the person doing something.

Use **me** when something happens to you.

I went to the zoo.

Tommy went with **me**.

I wanted something to drink.

Mother gave **me** a glass of milk.

Jose and **I** play ball after school.

The coach hit balls to Jose and **me**.

Using I & Me

Use the Word I

Rule
17

Write five things that you have done. Be sure to use the word **I**.

1. _____

_____

2. _____

_____

3. _____

_____

4. _____

_____

5. _____

_____

Name _____

A Game

Fill in the blanks with **I** or **me**.

1. Coach asked _____ to take the first kick.

2. _____ kicked the ball down the field.

3. _____ passed the ball to Tom.

4. Tom passed the ball back to _____.

5. _____ scored a goal!

6. The coach was proud of _____.

Name _____

My Dog

Fill in the blanks with **I** or **me**.

1. _____ take my dog for walks.

2. He chases _____.

3. _____ give him food.

4. He jumps on _____.

5. He licks _____ on the face.

6. _____ love it when he wags his tail.

Use **we** when you and other people do something.

Use **us** when something happens to you and other people.

We played jump rope at recess.

Tammy played with **us**.

We all yelled, "Surprise!"

The teacher gave **us** a big smile.

We make a mess when we cook.

Mother tells **us** to clean it up.

Using We & Us

Name _____

Use the Word We

Rule 18

Write five things that you and your friends do every day.
Use the word **we** to stand for **you and your friends**.

1. _____

_____

2. _____

_____

3. _____

_____

4. _____

_____

5. _____

_____

We or Us?

Fill in the blanks with **we** or **us**.

1. _____ are going to the store.

2. You can go with _____.

3. This is what _____ will make.

4. You can make it with _____.

5. Would you please sing with _____?

6. _____ will sing the song again.

7. Our teacher wants _____ to line up.

8. _____ should line up quickly.

The Recess

Write the best word in the blank.

1. _____ have fun at recess.
We   Us

2. _____ like to swing.
We   Us

3. The older kids play with _____.
we   us

4. _____ like to jump rope.
We   Us

5. All of _____ can jump ten times in a row.
we   us

6. _____ hope you will play with _____.
We   Us   we   us

Use **they** when several people do something.

Use **them** when something happens to several people.

> **They** made popcorn.
>
> Tina gave some of the popcorn to **them**.
>
> **They** went to the zoo.
>
> We went with **them**.
>
> Where did **they** go?
>
> We will hurry to catch **them**.

Using They & Them

They or Them?

Write the best word in the blank.

1. _____ are reading books.

They   Them

2. I would like to read books with _____.

they   them

3. My toes hurt. Please look at _____.

they   them

4. This is where _____ get off the bus.

they   them

5. _____ are playing on the swings.

They   Them

6. I know _____ would like ice cream.

they   them

7. I sit with _____ at lunchtime.

they   them

8. Here are ten pennies. You can count _____.

they   them

Toy Cars

Fill in the blanks with **they** or **them**.

1. I have many toy cars.

I play with _____ on Saturday.

2. My friends come over to play.

_____ like to play with my cars.

3. My cars are different colors.

_____ are blue, red, green, and yellow.

4. I like the red cars.

_____ look cool.

5. I gave some to my sister.

She likes _____, too.

Use They and Them

Write **they** or **them** in the blanks to answer the questions.

1. What do your fish do?

_____ can swim.

2. How many fish do you have?

I have two of _____.

3. What color are your fish?

_____ are gold.

4. Where do you keep your fish?

I keep _____ in a fishbowl.

5. When do you feed your fish?

I feed _____ every day.

Rule 20

Add **s** to most nouns to name more than one.

one	more than one
cat	cat**s**
dog	dog**s**
snake	snake**s**
shoe	shoe**s**
book	book**s**
train	train**s**

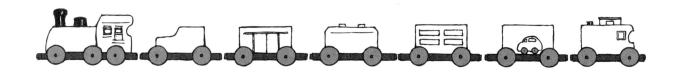

Plural Nouns

Name _____

How Many?

Rule
20

Label the pictures below. Tell how many and name the animals.

80

Name _____

More Than One

Change the word to mean **more than one**.

1. There were two _____ in the hall.

student

2. I have two pet _____.

frog

3. There are ten _____ in the toy box.

car

4. Four _____ jumped into the pool.

girl

5. I have collected one hundred _____.

rock

6. Here are your _____.

book

7. I like to eat _____.

cookie

8. All the _____ made honey.

bee

Name _____

Find the Plurals

Color each kite that names more than one thing.

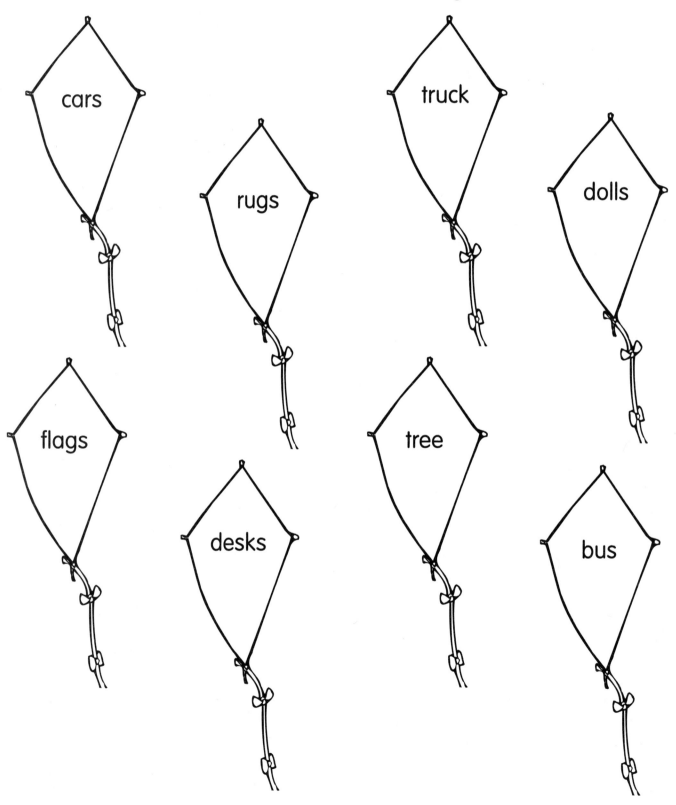

cars

truck

rugs

dolls

flags

tree

desks

bus

Rule 21

Add **es** to some nouns to show more than one.

one	more than one
box	box**es**
fox	fox**es**
dish	dish**es**
bush	bush**es**
ditch	ditch**es**
bench	bench**es**

Plural Nouns

More Than One

Add **s** or **es** to each noun to show **more than one**.

 sock_____

 comb_____

 shirt_____

 brush_____

 hat_____

 boot_____

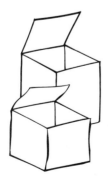 box_____

 dress_____

Make Plurals

Change the word to mean **more than one**.

1. I put all the _____ on the shelf.
dish

2. Mother bought a bunch of _____ .
radish

3. We have two _____ for our soccer team.
coach

4. Those _____ have puzzles in them.
box

5. Look at that family of _____.
fox

6. The students sat on five _____.
bench

7. We have a row of _____ in our yard.
bush

8. My snake is 25 _____ long.
inch

Add the Ending

Change the words to mean **more than one**.

1. one ax   two _____

2. one fox   two _____

3. one wish   two _____

4. one church   two _____

5. one branch   two _____

6. one dress   two _____

7. one bus   two _____

8. one kiss   two _____

9. one peach   two _____

Use **is** with one and **are** with more than one.

Jake **is** my friend.

Sam and Kim **are** friends.

The clock **is** ticking.

All the clocks **are** ticking.

Where **is** the pencil?

Where **are** the pencils?

Using Is & Are

Choose Is or Are

Fill in the blanks with **is** or **are**.

1. This _____ where my cat sleeps.

2. The cats _____ sleeping over there.

3. What _____ the students doing?

4. What _____ he doing?

5. These _____ your basketballs.

6. This _____ my basketball.

7. Where _____ he going?

8. Where _____ they going?

The Forest

Fill in the blanks with **is** or **are**.

1. The forest _____ a wonderful place.

2. The birds _____ flying.

3. There _____ trails to hike.

4. He _____ going to fish.

5. The wind _____ blowing.

6. The sun _____ shining.

7. We _____ sleeping in a tent.

8. There _____ stars in the sky.

Is or Are?

Write **is** or **are**.

1. There _____ a ball.

2. There _____ three red blocks.

3. There _____ a toy truck.

4. There _____ some crayons.

5. There _____ two books.

6. There _____ one key.

7. There _____ a picture.

8. There _____ four nickels.

       Grammar and Punctuation • EMC 2711

When something belongs to one person, add **'s** to the name of the person.

Jenny**'s** jacket

Dad**'s** truck

Pablo**'s** big dog

Cris**'s** red wagon

Possessives

Name _____

Whose Is It?

Rule 23

Label who each thing belongs to. Be sure to use an **'s**.

Whose Pet?

Tell who each pet belongs to.

1. Jan owns a cat.

_____ cat

2. Robin owns a bird.

_____ bird

3. Lee owns a frog.

_____ frog

4. Jeb owns a fish.

_____ fish

5. Amy owns a rabbit.

_____ rabbit

6. Cathy owns a turtle.

_____ turtle

The Name Game

Write a name in each blank to show who owns what.

1. Please don't eat _____ apple!

2. Has anyone seen _____ pencil?

3. Here is _____ notebook.

4. Is this _____ book?

5. That is _____ favorite picture.

6. This is _____ room.

7. Which one is _____ house?

8. Those are _____ papers.

Past or Present?

Write the best word in the blank.

Yesterday, the children _____ in the sand.
                          play played

Have you _____ the dog?
          walk walked

I like to _____ the flowers.
           pick picked

Have you _____ the math problem?
          finish finished

She _____ the ball down the hill.
     roll rolled

He likes to _____ the pencils on his desk.
             count counted

He _____ for his friend.
    wait waited

He _____ the gum all day.
    chew chewed

Rule 24

Some words add **ed** to tell
that something has already happ

jump**ed**	play**ed**	want**ed**
wash**ed**	rest**ed**	talk**ed**

Angelo **kicked** the ball past the goalie.

Mother **helped** us with our homework.

We **listened** to Father read us a book.

1. Y

2. F

3.

4.

5.

6.

7.

8.

Past Tense

What Happened?

Color the words that tell that something has already happened.

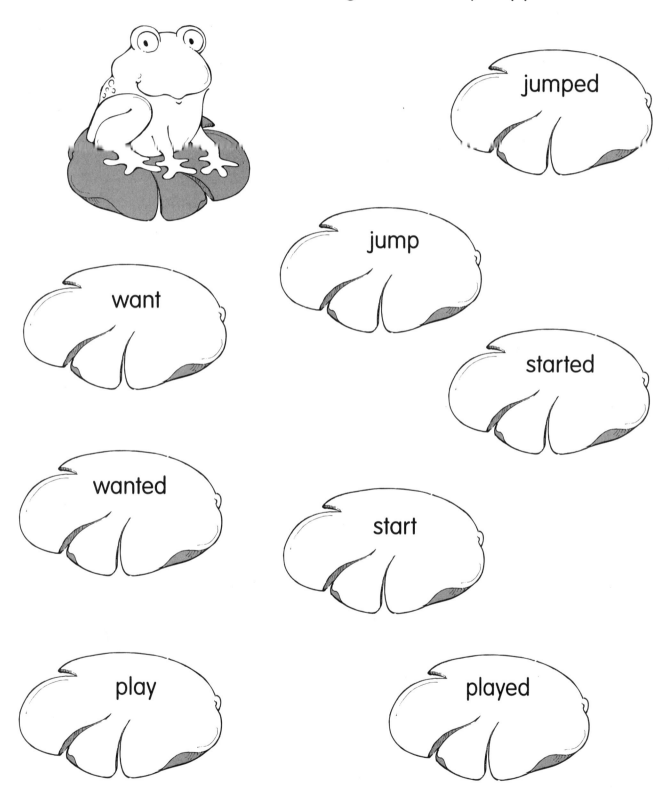

jumped

jump

want

started

wanted

start

play

played

In the Past

Change the word to mean that something has already happened.

1. The frog _____ into the pond.
    jump

2. The teacher _____ a question.
    ask

3. He _____ to play outside.
    want

4. Dan _____ around.
    turn

5. She _____ to a song.
    listen

6. Cindy _____ to read.
    start

7. The ladybug _____ across the leaf.
    crawl

8. He _____ everywhere for his library book.
    look

Some special words show that something has already happened.

ate	sang	came
caught	wrote	told

Mr. Ruiz **told** the class a story about a giant.

I **wrote** a letter to my pen pal in Africa.

The football player **caught** the ball.

Irregular Verbs

Past and Present

Circle the words that show that something has already happened.

1. do   did

2. gave   give

3. hide   hid

4. rang   ring

5. drew   draw

6. see   saw

7. fell   fall

8. run   ran

Now and Then

Write each word in the group where it belongs.

begin   began   take   took   rode   ride   feed   fed

is happening	has already happened
_____	_____
_____	_____
_____	_____

Hats

Color the words that tell that something has already happened.

Grammar and Punctuation Review
Part A, Rules 1–10
Fill in the bubble next to the correct answer.

A1. Which group of words is a sentence?
Ⓐ The tall boy.   Ⓑ The boy sang.

A2. Which group of words should begin with a capital letter?
Ⓐ my marker is red.   Ⓑ my red marker.

A3. Which sentence needs a period (.) at the end?
Ⓐ What are you doing
Ⓑ He jumped over the puddle

A4. Which sentence needs a question mark (?) at the end?
Ⓐ When are you going to see the movie
Ⓑ The movie was about a pony

A5. Which word should be capitalized in this sentence?
Ben and **i** read a **book** together.
             Ⓐ   Ⓑ

Fill in the bubble next to the word that should
begin with a capital letter.

A6. Ⓐ monkey   Ⓑ luis

A7. Ⓐ mexico   Ⓑ state

A8. Ⓐ day   Ⓑ friday

A9. Ⓐ july   Ⓑ month

A10. Ⓐ holiday   Ⓑ halloween

Name

Rule	Skill	Activity Pages			Review Questions		
		Circle when completed			Number	Correct	Not Correct
1	Identify complete sentences.	4	5	6	A1		
2	Capitalize the first word in sentences.	8	9	10	A2		
3	End telling sentences with a period.	12	13	14	A3		
4	End asking sentences with a question mark.	16	17	18	A4		
5	Capitalize the word *I*.	20	21	22	A5		
6	Capitalize names of people and pets.	24	25	26	A6		
7	Capitalize names of specific places.	28	29	30	A7		
8	Capitalize names of the days of the week.	32	33	34	A8		
9	Capitalize names of the months.	36	37	38	A9		
10	Capitalize names of holidays.	40	41	42	A10		
11	Identify nouns.	44	45	46	B1		
12	Identify verbs.	48	49	50	B2		
13	Identify pronouns.	52	53	54	B3		
14	Form contractions from two words.	56	57	58	B4		
15	Place apostrophes in contractions.	60	61	62	B5		
16	Identify compound words.	64	65	66	B6		
17	Use the words *I* and *me*.	68	69	70	B7		
18	Use the words *we* and *us*.	72	73	74	B8		
19	Use the words *they* and *them*.	76	77	78	C1		
20	Add *s* to make a noun plural.	80	81	82	C2		
21	Add *es* to make a noun plural.	84	85	86	C3		
22	Use the words *is* and *are*.	88	89	90	C4		
23	Add an apostrophe and *s* to show possession.	92	93	94	C5		
24	Add *ed* to form past tense forms of verbs.	96	97	98	C6		
25	Identify irregular past tense forms of verbs.	100	101	102	C7		

Notes to the Teacher

It may be appropriate for your class to expand the definition of a sentence.

A sentence has two parts:
- It names something.
- It tells what is happening.

With this expanded definition, it may help to use Rules 11 (nouns) and 12 (verbs) immediately after Rule 1.

Answer Key

Page 4

Items 1, 4, 5, and 7 should be circled.

Page 5

1. Mark fed his dog.
2. The dog chewed on a bone.
3. Ten students got on the bus.
4. Abby likes to read.
5. Everyone went outside to play.
6. Fred's frog jumped.

Page 6

Items 3, 4, 5, 6, and 8 should be colored.

Page 8

Items 1, 4, 5, 7, and 8 should be circled.
Items 2, 3, and 6 should be corrected.

Page 9

1. Her
3. The
5. Look
6. He
8. We

Page 10

1. yes
2. no
3. yes
4. yes
5. no
6. no
7. yes
8. no

Page 12

Items 1, 3, and 6 should have periods and be colored.

Page 13

1. Eric plays soccer.
2. I went to the zoo.
3. Sam planted sunflowers.
4. They can jump rope.

Page 14

1. He walked to school.
2. My dog eats a bone.
3. They like to play ball.
4. My friend's name is Sara.
5. She can ride a bike.
6. The clouds are in the sky.
7. My bike has two wheels.
8. Look at that pretty flower.

Page 16

1. ?	4. ?	7. ?
2. .	5. ?	8. .
3. .	6. ?	

Page 17

Asking Sentences	Telling Sentences
Do you have a pet mouse?	I have a pet mouse.
Would you like to play?	We can play a game.
Is your name Mike?	Your name is Mike.

Page 18

Items 1, 3, and 4 should end with a question mark. Statements will vary, but should respond to the question and end with a period.

Page 20

Items 1, 3, 6, and 7 should be circled.
Items 2, 4, 5, and 8 should be corrected with a capital *I*.

Page 21

Items 1 through 8 should have a capital *I* written in the blank.

Page 22

Items 1, 3, 4, and 5 should be colored.

Page 24

The following names should be capitalized:
Terry, Oscar, Carl.

Page 25

Names will vary, but should begin with capital letters.

Page 26

Names will vary, but should begin with capital letters.

Page 28

1. Central Park
2. Utah
3. Miami
4. The Great Mall
5. Main Street
6. Los Angeles Zoo
7. Disneyland
8. Amazon River

Page 29

Proper nouns will vary, but should begin with capital letters.

Page 30

The following words should be colored:
Ohio, Colorado, Sea World, Mexico, Chicago.

Page 32

In each sentence, the day of the week should be circled and capitalized.

Page 33

1. Sunday
2. Monday
3. Tuesday
4. Wednesday
5. Thursday
6. Friday
7. Saturday

Page 34

1. Wednesday
2. Saturday, Sunday
3. Friday
4. Monday
5. Tuesday, Thursday

Page 36

In each sentence, the month should be circled and capitalized.

Page 37

1. January, March
2. May
3. July, August
4. November

Page 38

1. Month will vary, but should begin with a capital letter.
2. May
3. June
4. January
5. December
6. Month will vary, but should begin with a capital letter.
7. June, July, or August
8. November

Page 40

These holidays should be circled and the capital letters underlined:
1. New Year's Day
2. Flag Day
3. Valentine's Day
4. Groundhog Day
5. Memorial Day
6. Martin Luther King, Jr. Day
7. Fourth of July
8. Labor Day

Page 41

1. Columbus Day
2. Kwanzaa
3. Veterans Day
4. Mother's Day
5. Earth Day
6. Father's Day
7. Halloween
8. Arbor Day

Page 42

1. Thanksgiving
2. Valentine's Day
3. St. Patrick's Day
4. Easter
5. Fourth of July
6. Halloween

Page 44
The following balloons should be colored:
book, table, frog, dime, banana.

Page 45
1. pig
2. ice cream
3. paper, desk
4. pencil
5. apple, bag
6. candy
7. flowers, table
8. shoes

Page 46
Nouns will vary, but should correctly
complete the sentences.

Page 48
Items 1, 2, 4, 5, 7, and 8 should
be colored.

Page 49
1. walks
2. ran
3. planted
4. chased
5. sang
6. sits
7. tells
8. sleeps

Page 50
1. barked
2. swim
3. ran or hopped
4. sat
5. drank
6. rode
7. read
8. hopped or ran

Page 52
1. He
2. They
3. She, it
4. We, them

Page 53
1. I
2. She or I
3. We or They
4. He or She
5. We or They
6. I
7. He or She
8. He or I

Page 54
1. She ate some cake.
2. They went to the lake.
3. He has a red boat.
4. We like to run.

Page 56

don't — can not
can't — let us
I'll — do not
wasn't — did not
it's — are not
didn't — I will
let's — was not
aren't — there is
there's — it is

Page 57
1. she's
2. that's
3. haven't
4. we'll
5. you'll
6. isn't
7. I've
8. they're

Page 58
1. did not
2. do not
3. it is
4. I will
5. could not
6. can not
7. he is
8. I am

Page 60

1. can't
2. it's
3. haven't
4. I'll
5. I've
6. he's
7. didn't
8. that's

Page 61

1. where's
2. what's
3. you've
4. we're
5. I'd
6. you're
7. isn't
8. I'm

Page 62

1. She's flying a kite.
2. What's your name?
3. They're having fun.
4. Please don't run in the house.
5. He doesn't ride the bus.

Page 64

1. football
2. skateboard
3. birthday
4. airplane
5. flashlight
6. something
7. everyone
8. doghouse

Page 65

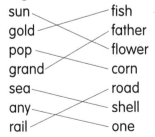

sun — fish
gold — father
pop — flower
grand — corn
sea — road
any — shell
rail — one

Page 66

afternoon   sidewalk
baseball   overnight
rainbow   everything

Page 68

Answers will vary, but should include the word *I*.

Page 69

1. me
2. I
3. I
4. me
5. I
6. me

Page 70

1. I
2. me
3. I
4. me
5. me
6. I

Page 72

Answers will vary, but should include the word *we*.

Page 73

1. We
2. us
3. we
4. us
5. us
6. We
7. us
8. We

Page 74

1. We
2. We
3. us
4. We
5. us
6. We, us

Page 76

1. They
2. them
3. them
4. they
5. They
6. they
7. them
8. them

Page 77
1. them
2. They
3. They
4. They
5. them

Page 78
1. They
2. them
3. They
4. them
5. them

Page 80

2 cats   4 dogs
3 bears   5 birds

Page 81
1. students
2. frogs
3. cars
4. girls
5. rocks
6. books
7. cookies
8. bees

Page 82

The following kites should be colored:
cars, rugs, dolls, flags, desks.

Page 84

socks   combs
shirts   brushes
hats   boots
boxes   dresses

Page 85
1. dishes
2. radishes
3. coaches
4. boxes
5. foxes
6. benches
7. bushes
8. inches

Page 86
1. axes
2. foxes
3. wishes
4. churches
5. branches
6. dresses
7. buses
8. kisses
9. peaches

Page 88
1. is
2. are
3. are
4. is
5. are
6. is
7. is
8. are

Page 89
1. is
2. are
3. are
4. is
5. is
6. is
7. are
8. are

Page 90
1. is
2. are
3. is
4. are
5. are
6. is
7. is
8. are

Page 92

Fido's   Ted's
Rob's   Lilly's

Page 93
1. Jan's cat
2. Robin's bird
3. Lee's frog
4. Jeb's fish
5. Amy's rabbit
6. Cathy's turtle

Page 94
Names will vary, but should end with an 's.

Page 96
1. played
2. walked
3. pick
4. finished
5. rolled
6. count
7. waited
8. chewed

Page 97
The following words/lily pads should be colored: jumped, wanted, started, played.

Page 98
1. jumped
2. asked
3. wanted
4. turned
5. listened
6. started
7. crawled
8. looked

Page 100
1. did
2. gave
3. hid
4. rang
5. drew
6. saw
7. fell
8. ran

Page 101
is happening:
begin
take
ride
feed

has already happened:
began
took
rode
fed

Page 102
The following words/hats should be colored: went, rang, came, knew.

Grammar and Punctuation Review

Part A	Part B	Part C
A1. B	B1. B	C1. B
A2. A	B2. A	C2. A
A3. B	B3. B	C3. B
A4. A	B4. B	C4. B
A5. A	B5. B	C5. A
A6. B	B6. A	C6. B
A7. A	B7. A	C7. A
A8. B	B8. B	
A9. A		
A10. B		

Language Fundamentals
Grade 1
Sample Pages

A **noun** is a naming word.

A noun can name a person, place, animal, or thing.

person: The **boy** runs fast.   **animal:** The **cat** naps.

place: The **school** is open.   **thing:** The **hat** is red.

Look at the picture. Read the words. Fill in the circle next to the noun.

1.

○ run   ○ boy

2.

○ park   ○ open

3.

○ jump   ○ dog

4.

○ book   ○ read

Name _____

A **noun** is a naming word.

A noun can name a person, place, animal, or thing.

person: The **girl** is tall.　　**animal:** The **cat** is black.

place: The **store** is big.　　**thing:** The **toy** is small.

Read the sentence.
Draw a line from the sentence to the picture.
The first one has been done for you.

1. I see the sun. – – – – – – – – –

2. There is a tall tree.

3. There is a blue slide.

4. Look at the boy run!

5. I see a red bird.

A **common noun** names a person, place, animal, or thing. A common noun begins with a lowercase letter.

Person	Place	Animal	Thing
girl	school	bird	book
man	home	pig	shoe
friend	library	dog	boat
doctor	park	cow	apple

Read the sentence. Underline the common noun and write it on the line.

1. This is the school.   _____

2. Here is my friend.   _____

3. Where is a cookie?   _____

4. Ask the teacher.   _____

5. The cat ate it!   _____

Write to finish the sentence.

6. A _____ noun names a person, place, animal, or thing.

CCLS 1.1b Use Common Nouns   Language Fundamentals • EMC 2881 • © Evan-Moor Corp.

A **common noun** can name a person.

My **mother** likes to cook.   Your **friend** is nice.
The **boy** rides a bike.   The **dentist** may be late.

Read the sentence. Underline the common noun
that names a person. Write the noun on the line.

1. Did the teacher have a toy?   _____

2. The baby likes the toy.   _____

3. The girl likes to play, too.   _____

4. Her brother fell down!   _____

5. The father can help.   _____

6. Can the doctor help?   _____

Write a common noun that names a person.

7. _____

A **common noun** can name a place.

> We go to the **park**.   We buy food at the **store**.
> The **house** is small.   We ride our bikes to the **corner**.

Read the sentence. Underline the common noun
that names a place. Write the noun on the line.

1. Where is the zoo?   _____

2. We live by the school.   _____

3. I walk to the park.   _____

4. The playground is fun.   _____

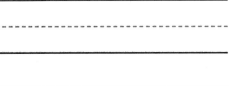

5. I can see the river.   _____

6. Do you see the street?   _____

Write a common noun that names a place.

7. _____

A **common noun** can name an animal or thing.

Animal	Thing
The **cat** sleeps.	I have a **book**.
The **cow** looks for grass.	The **car** goes fast.
The green **frog** can hop.	Is that my **milk**?

Read the sentence. Underline the common noun that names an animal or thing. Write the noun on the line.

1. Can you see the boat? _____

2. It is on the water. _____

3. There is a whale! _____

4. Is that a yellow bird? _____

5. The sea has a lot to see. _____

Write a common noun that names an animal.

6. _____